I had really intended to illustrate the old classic story of Reynard the Fox— that would have kept me busily entertained all winter,

but unfortunately that didn't work out.

I had been looking forward
to it quite a bit because
I like to draw
animals —

especially the fox!

In the delightful tale of
this rascal's tricks there
are many opportunities
for me to draw the fox.

In doing so I could have used
the knowledge I've gathered
during the cold winter
evenings in the woods when,
from high up in a big
tree, I've observed my
ruddy friend.

The lion and the bear, which also frequently appear in the story, are my nearby neighbors in the zoo in Amersfoort.

This dead wolf was given to me for study by the Burgers Zoo.

Now I can observe the surly fellow as closely as I like.

Then there is Tibeert the cat,

Cuvaart the hare,

Cortois the dog,

Grimbeert the badger,

Tiecelin the raven,

Merlin the monkey.

So far everything is just fine

but when I discovered Belin the ram → in a meadow along Wieksloter Road

I realized immediately that I was going to be in trouble.

In the story the ram carries a shopping bag, reads prayers from a book, and does all kinds of things like that for which its body is not really suitable →

With a monkey and a bear I can do pretty well, but it is impossible to draw a realistic picture of a horse pouring a cup of tea.

And a drawing of Chanticleer the rooster carrying a stretcher seems somewhat awkward.

And something else still:

this is how we picture a wolf

but as soon as he stands on his hind legs he loses some of that essence of a wolf.

Also, as far as facial expressions are concerned,
it becomes apparent that you can't just do
whatever you like:

a lion that
looks serious,

a bear
with a
look of a
simpleton,

and a
hypocritical-
looking fox

all these are
easy to do because   these characteristics are
already in their nature to a certain extent,

but when faced
with a giggling badger
or an indignant rabbit, they
begin to look too much like
Donald Duck cartoon figures for me

And then there is that troublesome question:
do they wear clothes or don't they?

No, the longer I think about it
for this story there is nothing
better than those original
and charming woodcuts. ⟶

So
we take the bull
by the horns

and tap
up a new
barrel—

We are
starting a

dog
book

Dogs

HARRY N. ABRAMS, INC., PUBLISHERS, NEW YORK

The first portrait will be of course
our good old SEP

or GROSSE SE SIÊUWS, or NOF,

as our sons called him in their children's language.
It doesn't matter to him which of his
names we use to address him, since
in the meantime he has become
rather deaf.

When we want to get his
attention, we just stamp
our feet.

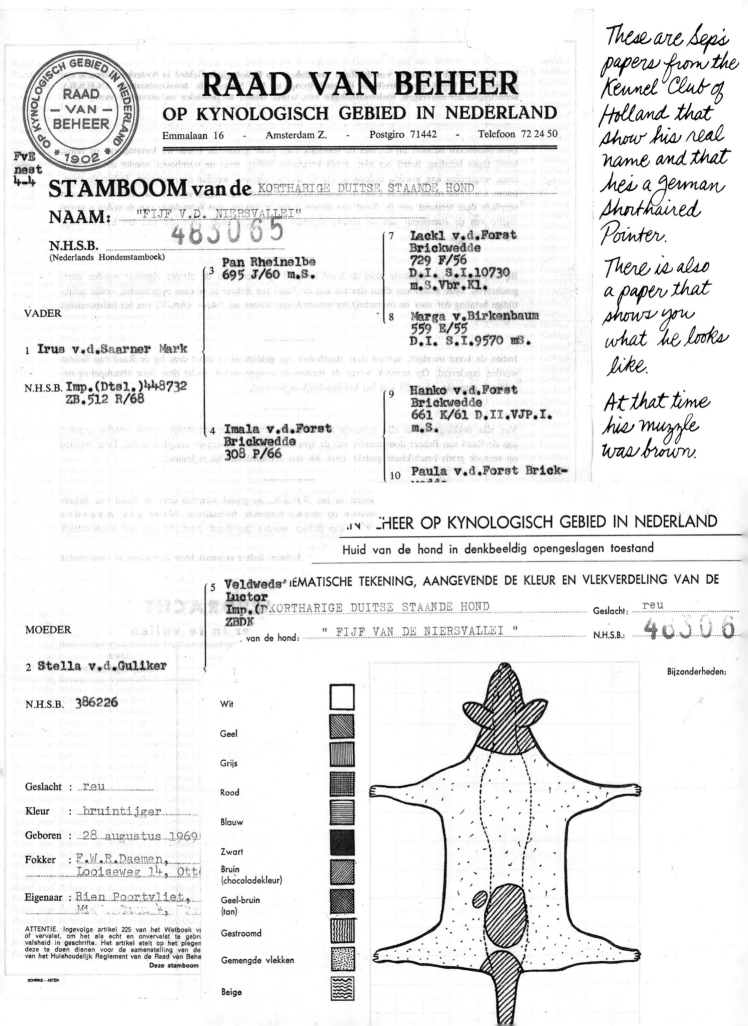

RAAD VAN BEHEER
OP KYNOLOGISCH GEBIED IN NEDERLAND

Emmalaan 16 - Amsterdam Z. - Postgiro 71442 - Telefoon 72 24 50

RAAD
- VAN -
BEHEER
OP KYNOLOGISCH GEBIED IN NEDERLAND
* 1902 *

FvE
nest
4-4

STAMBOOM van de KORTHARIGE DUITSE STAANDE HOND

NAAM: "FIJF V.D. NIERSVALLEI"

N.H.S.B.   485065
(Nederlands Hondenstamboek)

VADER

1 **Irus v.d.Saarner Mark**

N.H.S.B. Imp.(Dtsl.)448732
ZB.512 R/68

3 Pan Rheinelbe
695 J/60 m.S.

4 Imala v.d.Forst
Brickwedde
308 P/66

7 Lackl v.d.Forst
Brickwedde
729 F/56
D.I.S.I.10730
m.S.Vbr.Kl.

8 Marga v.Birkenbaum
559 E/55
D.I.S.I.9570 mS.

9 Hanko v.d.Forst
Brickwedde
661 K/61 D.II.VJP.I.
m.S.

10 Paula v.d.Forst Brick-

MOEDER

2 **Stella v.d.Guliker**

N.H.S.B. 386226

5 Veldweds*
Luctor
Imp.(
ZBDK

Geslacht : reu

Kleur : bruintijger

Geboren : 28 augustus 1969

Fokker : F.W.R.Daemen,
Looiseweg 14, Ott

Eigenaar : Rien Poortvliet,

HEER OP KYNOLOGISCH GEBIED IN NEDERLAND

Huid van de hond in denkbeeldig opengeslagen toestand

EMATISCHE TEKENING, AANGEVENDE DE KLEUR EN VLEKVERDELING VAN DE
KORTHARIGE DUITSE STAANDE HOND   Geslacht: reu

van de hond: " FIJF VAN DE NIERSVALLEI "   N.H.S.B.: 485065

Bijzonderheden:

Wit

Geel

Grijs

Rood

Blauw

Zwart

Bruin
(chocoladekleur)

Geel-bruin
(tan)

Gestroomd

Gemengde vlekken

Beige

During the day
I sit for long periods
working in a rather uncomfortable
position because Sep lies snoring under
my table and I can't put my feet there.

Oh well, he's such a good old soul
I just let him be
until his passing gas gets really
too bad.
Then he has to go — come on,
get going!
He gets to his feet and trudge
off to the living room.

It's not always easy to get those old bones up on the couch. He is particularly slow if he has been out hunting the day before with Tok, my son. But he's always determined to go.

Just as soon as Tok or I happen to put on a hunting-type jacket or work boots for a little job in the yard, Sep immediately assumes that we are planning to sneak off and go hunting <u>without him</u>, and starts howling, sky-high!

No matter how old and stiff he has become,
retrieving a duck or a pigeon
is still one of his
greatest joys!

Out of respect for his age we take the
old fellow along,
and then try to arrange matters so
that the downed pigeon does not fall
in a wheat field or on the far side
of a ditch.
Sometimes we even have to point
out to him where the pigeon
has fallen.
Oh well, we don't mind.

When he finds
the pigeon or duck
he brings it back
with such dignity
and grace!

The way in which he calmly accepts my praise,
looking away with a refined air,
would really make you think that
you are dealing with an experienced
and composed hunting dog! →

And indeed there are days
when Sep does a nice job,
but just as often he drives
me crazy.

A trick he frequently played on me was
to run off and disappear instead of
retrieving the pigeon (which should be
located somewhere around here).

Meanwhile you
would hear him
howling somewhere
very far away
while chasing a hare

He'd come stumbling back,
looking guilty, half an hour later, and
would drop down like a limp dishrag.

He was so exhausted that he
couldn't do a thing more.

We've often threatened Sep with the
punishment of later
having him stuffed
to look very ugly!

Sep has never seemed to understand selective hunting. Roebucks that I'd let pass by without a shot excited him so much that he'd violently tug at the leash, barking away. Rolling about in the sand, nearly choking himself, he would protest so fiercely that people on the other side of the hunting ground thought that someone was kicking his dog.

Also, Sep has never seen the point of uselessly observing game.

To think that 12 years have passed since Sep came to us like a small surprise package.

AARDEWERK

At night we kept him in a box next to my bed, and he would squeal, scratch, and lick my face.

In the dark of the night I'd take him downstairs — in case he had to urinate.

But he'd just sit right by the door and shiver. ....

OK, back into the box... and again, and again.

← trying to toilet train him

teaching him to get used to the leash

Making him understand all the things that are allowed and those that aren't.

There are all kinds of things a young dog has to learn, and even more that a hunting dog needs to know.

This is the correct place the dog should be when you want him to heel — not pulling forward and not lagging behind.

And when the master suddenly stops, the dog should sit down without any command to do so.

It is clear that these mistakes would not meet the requirements of the obedience training tests.

In the old days the obedience trials had to be passed or else you couldn't keep your dog.

Sep and I have gone over the rule book thoroughly.

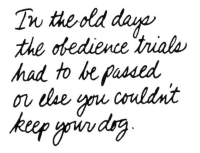

One job to which we devoted an enormous amount of time: heeling properly.

In order to teach him not to walk too far to the side,

And to teach him not to walk too far forward, I would make a sudden turn to the left

I would pass by a tree without any room to spare.

And then there is "down"!

The dog must remain lying down in this position even if his master walks off.

First we do it this way and later on like this

Practicing with the retrieval block.

HOLD ON!

And to keep things in proportion we have to let the dog have his way every so often.

And so, with paint on his paw, Sep has put his signature here.

Another beloved companion — an old
sausage of almost twelve years —
is our wirehaired Dachshund

MAX
also called WOKS

a quiet, friendly, intelligent,
stubborn character —

and obviously
too fat.
↓

We have never been able to do anything about that. He is simply too sharp and manages to steal some of the other dogs' food.

hen you throw a
andful of biscuits on
he floor, most dogs
ll bolt down what
ey can;
t not Max;
  he grabs as many
  as he can hold
    in his mouth and then disappears.

Max is the kind who takes his own sweet time.
He obstinately will not walk one bit faster...
even if a bull were to come after him.

The look on
that face!

He's able to get up a slow gallop, but only if he feels like it — not so bad for an old dog.

The day before yesterday I saw a Dachshund of 16!

He was still in excellent health.

If luck is with us we will have a lot of fun with Max for some time come. He's fine as long as he does not get backaches — he has have an injection n the pain.

And for a long while afterward he still suffers.

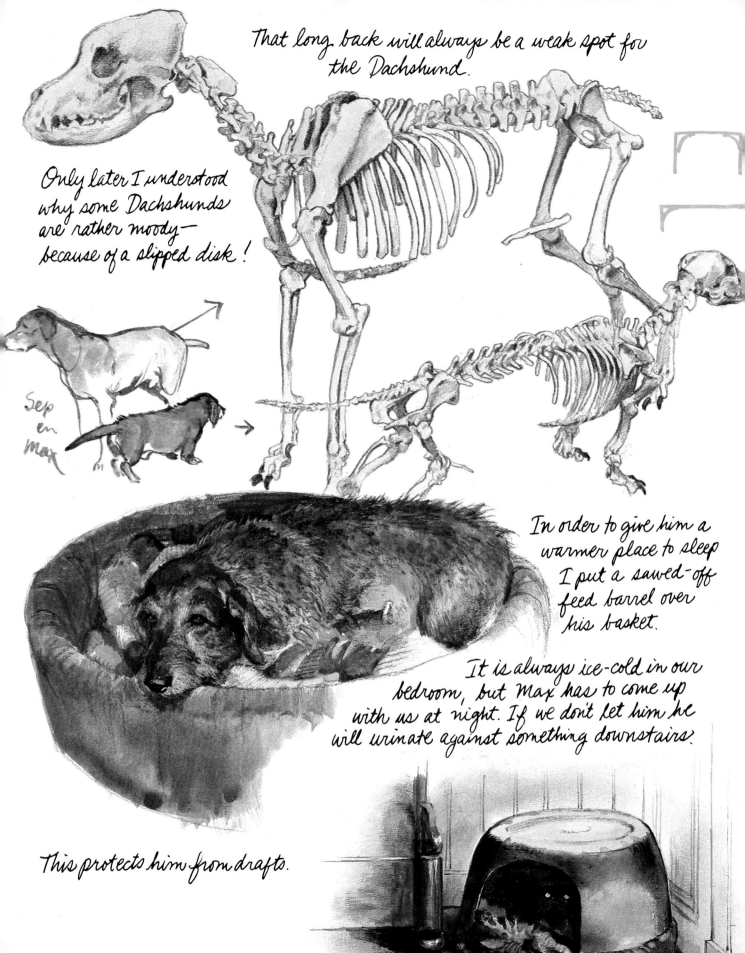

That long back will always be a weak spot for the Dachshund.

Only later I understood why some Dachshunds are rather moody— because of a slipped disk!

Sep en Max

In order to give him a warmer place to sleep I put a sawed-off feed barrel over his basket.

It is always ice-cold in our bedroom, but Max has to come up with us at night. If we don't let him he will urinate against something downstairs.

This protects him from drafts.

The real job of the wirehaired Dachshund is to trail game and bring the animal to ← a standstill.

But somehow I don't see Max doing this, with his not-a-bit-faster attitude. No, it would end up more like this. ↓

the only game I ever saw Max corner →

I remember another one of his heroic deeds.

Max hates it when my wife is away from home.

He waits in the window until she comes back.

Max brought home a myxomatose rabbit that was still alive. And since there was nobody else home my wife had to put the poor thing out of its misery!

a jolly mood →

a tuft of Max's hair ←

The third member of
the club is our
five-year-old
Jack Russell terrier,
called

TIMOTHEUS
(also Tim or Pielie)

He's a brisk and intelligent young chap, and almost nothing
escapes him. He is at his sharpest when he is hunting
mice, and he's already caught huge numbers of them.

Tim is always busy
hunting in one place or
another around the yard,
so there's no chance a
newly arrived rat or mouse
will ever get a resident's
permit.

No matter what job I'm doing out in the yard, Tim will be there, at my heels, because you never know...

as soon as I bend down to pick up a board or something, those piercing black eyes are already searching: mice?

At the pile of old roof tiles against the barn, Tim will stand barking and whining for so long that it gets to be a nuisance, and we must call him back.

Tim's coat is made up of long, white, stiff goatlike hairs.

dog tired and dirty

d this is **MANASSE** or *Noesj*. He is also a Jack Russell. In spite of his youthful appearance he is three years old.

the display of power from Tim, when Manasse came for the first time

They are almost always together, and Tim still rules the roost.

On Mondays and Thursdays the trash is collected, a treat for the terriers because they get to accompany me to the road

and again at night when I bring the cans back.

Each dog has his own pecularities:

This is Sep's typical pose, with those behind legs spread out.

This is the way Manasse always stretches.

Tim likes to rub himself on the mat.

Max bangs his nose full force against the floor when he sneezes.

We have been lucky with our dogs: they are all nice fellows who not only get along well together, but also with the other animals.

← Ko

They simply ignored the strange bird Kees Oorbeek, a kestrel who lived with us for a year in order to recuperate.

It is particularly mystifying that they barely notice the duck that flew in as a total stranger... and to think that Sep loves to retrieve them!

—

The chickens also have nothing to fear from the dogs. (the eggs do: Sep likes to scoop them up out of the coops; that's why I built a little fence here.)

But their patience has its limits — they hate it when cats come in the yard.

I don't want to be unkind, but when good old Sep someday passes away we probably won't get another German Shorthaired Pointer. I think that too much passion for the hunt has been bred into this stock. I also think that after Max goes we will not have another wirehaired Dachshund — we have been lucky with this good old soul, and chances are small that we will ever find another like him.

Although we've come to prefer the German Wirehaired Pointer, it won't hurt to consider another breed.

And when that time comes— let's be honest, we should know by then what kind of dog we want.

In any case it will have to be a hunting dog who wants to retrieve,

and we would like him to have the looks of a watchdog who could scare off possible evildoers,

not a growling fearsome fellow who scares everyone.

There is not enough work in our yard for a real police dog— we just don't get enough robbers paying us a visit.

Neither should he be a softy who just stands there wagging his tail like a simpleton.

It just so happens
that Robbiecomefront
passed his exam
this week.

bringing the
robber along,
which is called
the transport
↓

Robbiecomefront is
the dog that belongs to
the young policeman who
often uses the alleys arou
our house for training.
Sometimes he manages
to scare me.

I'll be peacefully
walking around outside
when all of a sudden there
is a roar from somewhere
behind the bushes.

Robbiecomefront !!!

It scares me to death every time.

This was one tense moment:
keeping a sharp eye on the
robber, Robbiecomefront did
not notice that on the sly
a pistol was dropped.
↙ That cost him a few points,
but the certificate was
obtained anyway.

Isn't there a chance that a dog might learn to go after that jacket mainly?

Then the problem will be that a criminal dressed in everyday clothing will be able to go quietly about his business,

while an innocent fat man in such a jacket would become the target!

I imagine that it is mainly those three horizontal lines that make it happen!

I have a pair of pajamas of just about the same loose cut and with some of those "carpet-beaters" sewed on.

For someone who is watching for one, it looks pretty much like that practice robber's jacket..!

I might be going out in my pajamas one summer morning to get the paper from the mailbox,

and Robbiecomefront might be doing some practicing here in the neighborhood...

An excellent dog for the police but not quite right I think as a "garden variety" pet.

In order to get to know better
all the different breeds, I'll draw
some of them.
It's hard to love what you
don't know, and this way we can
learn a thing or two.

That's enough of the breeds for now!

The dog-tax collector estimates the number
of dogs in our village to be about 4,000.

Taxes have been paid for 2,845 dogs
(including Sep, Max, Tim, and Manasse,
unfortunately).

The remaining dogs are left for him to "catch."

How do they actually do that anyhow—
that "catching"?

does the municipality, in addition
to the ordinary informers, also
have informers who secretly follow
people walking their dogs to their
homes and then write down their addresses?

I think this dog-
tax business is
awfully silly.

POORTVLIET

We have to pay the village of Soest 310 guilders ($115) a year for dogs that never
leave the yard: two old ones that stroll stiffly around the house and two
small terriers that hide little turds as small as cigar butts in our own closed-
wooded area in front of the house!
I just went over to look for some under the bushes:
I found one!

actual
size

It is logical that you pay less road tax
for a small car than for a full-sized
one — but for the accountant
of the municipality
there is no
difference:

dog remains dog.

I am going
to visit some
more dogs.

Now that I've done it,
I don't think much
of all those dog
breeds together
on one page.
I will do it
   differently now—
one by one in oil paint.
Here's a strong and
friendly sled dog:
the Siberian Husky.

The Alaskan
Malamute
has something
of the same
posture as
the Husky.

The
sixteen-
year-old
Dachshund!

a Belgian dog:
the Belgian Malinois
← (an old one)
I once had such
a dog.

the
neighbors'
German
Shepherd

This dog is easy
to train:
a Belgian Sheepdog,

the Groenendael.

This roguish fellow
is a Briard, a fine
old breed of sheepdog
from France.

When they are black they
look rather like a
Bouvier.

Height : 22-27 inches

another well-known
sheepdog, the Collie

A very nice dog is the exceptionally smart Border Collie.

The Shetland Sheepdog
might be described
as a small Collie.

The Kuvasz is
a white, robust
dog from Hungary.

This hairy cattle dog is
an Old English sheepdog,
also known as the Bobtail.

The Welsh Corgi (Pembroke) is a small cattle dog 10-12 inches high.

Their size is rather convenient, because it sometimes happens that when they drive the cattle, an angry cow kicks back — but that blow just slides past the dog.

It's really almost too much... dogs that are big-small, fat-thin, high-low, shorthaired-longhaired, and then all kinds of colors too!

It's amazing that even the smallest child knows enough to call each one of these different-looking animals "dog"!

A cat and a rabbit are more alike than these two...

... and this dog, in addition to all those many other breeds, actually descends from the wolf!

It is almost unbelievable!

t first sight
ere aren't
any wolflike
    characteristics!

↓

It must have been a tremendous piece of good luck for early man when, nosing about for food, he happened upon a litter of young animals. It was a much easier way to find food than cornering a vicious bear!

So a litter of wolf pups would gratefully have been taken home, intended to be the family's next meal.

But perhaps a whining child finagled it so that one of these cuddly pups would stay alive, and maybe they discovered that having such a companion around the house wasn't a bad idea.

It warned you when something was wrong

and was good for tracking down wild animals.

So maybe we came together this way..

It's difficult to see a resemblance between these two pairs.
↓ A few thousand years separate them.
And as time went on, some of
the talents of the ancestor wolf
did not disappear

because here is the "wolf"
again at work thousands
of years later ↓

as a Hanoverian
Haidbracke,
tracking game...

as a Pointer on point,
indicating the location
of the game,

here as an English Setter,

as the elegant Irish Setter
(related to the English and Gordon Setters)
I see passing by with its master every day,

as a brave Wachtelhund

and as Sep
retrieving.

chasing a hare

What do you think
of this brave
wirehaired
Dachshund?

The task of this
Norwegian Elkhound
is to keep the elk
there until the
others arrive.

This house dog looks after home and premises.

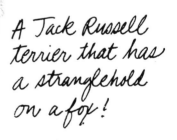

A Jack Russell terrier that has a stranglehold on a fox!

The nerve of such a little thing to dive straight into that dark tunnel and then attack the fox right there!

up a minute for some air and then down again.

Think of facing something like this in a narrow tube —

It won't be the first time that a small dog like this strangles the fox in its own den!

The sheepdog skillfully maneuvers
the flock to where he wants it—

the same talent with which
the wolf separates an animal
from the herd as his prey—
not one more movement than
necessary, and above all
no panic!

The Border Collie
in a typical
↓ crouching position.

He always cleverly
blocks the way,
knowing precisely how
such a stupid herd animal
will react.
A talent like this
must be
inherited.

The act of retrieving / fetching downed game and carrying it to the master.

is actually similar to dragging food to the den...

as the wolf still does,
here with a wood grouse

As Sep brings me a duck, it doesn't look much different, either.

I've been looking
for various
breeds at the
houses of friends
and acquaintances.

the clever
Pointer

the Cocker Spaniel,
a little gun dog
that owes its name to
woodcock and
cock pheasant

This is the American
Cocker Spaniel.

The English Springer Spaniel
is a smart hunting dog
that is not bothered
by thorns, etc,
because of its thick coat.

This worried-looking
creature is the
Basset Hound.

The Smooth
Fox Terrier
is a keen little
rat catcher.

This is
the
shaggy
variety, the
Wire Fox Terrier,
with hair that really
feels like wire.

For the dog show its
mustache is combed
forward.
I just tried this
on myself—
it feels unpleasant.

I will continue on for a
while with the terriers.
This is the Bull Terrier,
originally bred for dogfighting.

Actually, it resembles the Bulldog
more than it does the real terrier type.

This happy
silhouette is the
Scottish Terrier.

These charming
little dogs are a
breed I'd like
someday to possess:
the Cairn Terrier.

The terrier that might have
gotten some of its looks
from the greyhound
is the Bedlington.

A little dog you often see
with a silly little knot of
ribbons on its head
(though that is something
it cannot help) is the
Yorkshire Terrier.

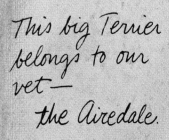

This big Terrier belongs to our vet—
the Airedale.

These little playthings are young
West Highland White Terriers.

I love to watch when people greet a puppy—you can immediately tell whether or not they're "dog people."

For something like
this you should
bend down
(think of the cuddle
circles of the gnomes!).

Look here—
this of course means
that this man has
← never had a dog and will never own one.

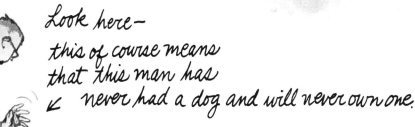

A thing you also sometimes see:
someone tries to be nice and
wants to pet the dog, but
because of those jaws, only on
the back of the head.
Just because it all happens so
awkwardly the dog looks up…

and then there is that frightened withdrawal of the hand!

brother and
sister with
Labrador pups

an old-fashioned
little dog, the
Wachtelhund

The Drentse Partridge Dog
is a Dutch breed.

The dogs you'd expect to see in an old painting:
the large Münsterländers

*beautiful, strong
and friendly dogs:
Golden Retrievers
Height: 21½ - 24 inches*

This one too seems
to me to be a
nice dog.
The Hanoverian
Haidbracke is a
tracking dog;
its job is to find
the wounded game.

wirehaired
and
longhaired Dachshunds

The Wachtelhund is a spaniel-like dog with an excellent nose that serves him well when following game.

Height: 18 inches

The German Pointer
comes in shorthaired and wirehaired varieties.

This is the Wirehaired.
Height: 22-26 inches

This is, I think
a fine dog.
I would like to have one like this.

How we teach the dog to dance to our tune!
We put it in front of our carriage,

and under our carriage,
and behind it,

we ask it to pull the travois,

and the sled.

It has to keep watch over us, guide us,

rescue us,

and we want it to defend us, show us where gas is escaping or where drugs are hidden, lead us in the direction the villain has gone...

and it does it all.

It looks after cattle,

points out where the game is hidden,

cleverly urges the ducks to the decoy, if necessary,

calls its master when it has found the buck,

and is still willing to sit up and give a paw—

as if all that were not enough.

A pretty and clever little dog, its work is to lure the ducks: the Dutch Decoy Dog.

the Beagle,
a dog with a pleasant appearance

A breed that was officially extinct,

but that was bred back aga
is the Dutch Smousdog!

It's a cheerful little dog
that deserves to be here again.

sketches of the Hungarian
Pointer, the Viszla
(nice dog)

Zarah,
a Basenji

Afghan Hound

The dog that runs the courses
at incredible speeds is
the Greyhound.

Borzoi,
a dog from Russia

(Think of all the places our
dogs come from:
Belgium, Germany, France,
England, Hungary.
Afghanistan, Austria, to name a few.)

a product of crossbreeding
the St. Bernard,
Pyrenean Mountain Dog,
and the Newfoundland:
the Leonberger

The Pyrenean Mountain Dog
weighs 90-125 pounds.
(In the United States it's the Great Pyrenees
and is usually white.)

a group of arctic dogs
I happened to meet
on the street:

Samoyeds

a Bouvier des Flandres
living in our
neighborhood.

I heard a story about a Bouvier that is supposed to be true.

A woman returns home and finds that her Bouvier is coughing and choking.

Has he swallowed a little bone or something?

Matters do not improve so a vet is called and, ah yes, after some fumbling he gets hold of the thing that was bothering the dog: two fingers!

Bewilderment prevails. Police are all over, investigating, questioning the neighbors, etc. When a cupboard in the hall is opened, there is a man, bloody and unconscious. ← A burglar.

I imagine it happened like this: suddenly the black dog rushes into the hallway after the thief.

"No, down!" There was only a second to get into the cupboard.

Our vet also had a story like that. An otherwise friendly bloodhound bit off two fingers when someone stuck his hand through the mail slot.

the Brussels Griffon,
a small dog 12 inches high

"Oh, a little French Bulldog," I said.

"No, a Boston Terrier," they said. If you know that it has happened more than once that these dogs have gotten confused, then it's not that stupid.

From this white part you can see how much more of a nose, for instance, the Welsh Corgi has.

French Bulldog

English Bulldog.

a pretty grumpy-looking
character indeed
but still an honest fellow
with a friendly nature

St. Bernard

The Bernese
Mountain Dog,
like the St. Bernard,
comes from Switzerland.

the enormous
Neapolitan
Mastiff

The Doberman Pinscher was
"invented" in Germany in around
1890 by Ludwig Dobermann, who
wanted a good guard dog.

This is the black variety;
they also come in
dark chocolate brown.

Height:
up to 33 inches!

This is the
Great Dane,
which all Germans
call the
"German Dane."
It's a pity that a dog
like this does not
have a long life.

Another robust dog is
the strong and watchful
Rottweiler.

the Dalmatian,
the dog that
goes with horses
and carriages

There is the
       Giant Schnauzer
(height: 23½–27½ inches);

the Standard ———→
       (17–19 inches);
and the Miniature
       (12–14 inches).

Boxer pups

I was thinking yesterday evening in bed:
who could possibly have been the first person to decide to take
scissors and change a puppy according to his own idea
of how it should look? Snip a piece from each ear,
a piece from the tail....
That man must have had a wife or
a brother — what did they have
to say about this?

In the meantime we've gotten used to it,
but doesn't it seem silly to cut the little parts
from an animal if we think them inappropriate?
Such jokes on a private hedge seem all right
to a point.

Maybe somebody thinks that a
hare like this is nice;

and what about this tail that is
much too
long ?

And these big things— aren't they just asking for the hedge trimmers?

I honestly don't understand why they crop the ears of the Great Dane, for instance,

and not the Mastiff

or the Rottweiler.

Boxers

Our first dog was a Boxer.

I can strongly recommend a Boxer to families with young children.

Amber

"Yes, but they do slobber," some people might say.

This is true only when you teach it to beg for food because that causes its mouth to water — just like us when we pass the Chinese restaurant. If we had those low corners on our mouth we would drool too.

That's how it is.

A dog in the house is such fun for the childre There is a lot that the poor animal must tolerate!
Between the bars of the crib, ears are pulled, eyes are poked, etc., etc.

And, oh dear. if the poor soul accidently knocks down some Lego structures or bites a leak in the ball, it's always "that rotten dog"!

Only when the children become older
do they fully appreciate
the dog.

hey discover
w willing an audience
e can be when they
n't want to tell their
ubles to anyone else.

He comforts and listens —
think of all
that gets
whispered in
a dog's ear!

URBAN

These qualities
should certainly not
be underestimated.

One of the funniest dog experiences I ever had was when I was walking with Amber and small Urban on a dim and misty evening. All of a sudden a bevy of about 15 owls swooped down without a sound on the young dog. I dashed up swinging the leash at them... and everything disappeared into the haze!

Here are a couple of old sketches of Amber and Urban.

Amber and Urban were nice dogs, just a little stupid, but then they couldn't help that. They were uneasy with other dogs and also with foreigners. To them, a Turk learning to ride a bike was like a red flag to a bull. At Christmas they also hated Saint Nicholas' helper, Black Peter. (He should have thought better of it before he put sweets in the shoes the children put out for Saint Nick, because the candy was long gone by morning.)

In fact they didn't like anything out of the ordinary. I remember a pedestrian who had a loose sole on his shoe, and with each step he pulled his leg up in a rather odd way. Then you had to take a firm stand with those dogs!

KLAP

Once we met a stray cow on the street while taking an evening walk. I wanted to return it, so I untied the dogs because I needed the leash, and requested that they go nicely "down."

Pretending a lack of interest, I approached the cow and was just about to tie the leash around its horns when the animal tore off—straight through the small gardens of some newly built houses. I succeeded in dashing past the cow and then spread my arms wide to head it off.

Seeing this, Amber and Urban decided to take action.

Immediately it became a complete madhouse—growling dogs, panicking cow, and all of them running through the hedges.

Out of one garden, into the next.

I was able to prevent a rabbit hutch from being crushed, but five gardens for sure were lost. Finally, we left the situation as it was and slunk away, the three of us — how silly we looked.

th Urban we had a lot of trouble. I remember one evening, during a severe
nter, we had walked to the Poldervaart,

looking for half-frozen waterbirds,
so we could help them
(not that Boxers are
skillful retrievers, but
they did spot the
birds).

Urban was chasing some
poor coot when he disappeared
from sight!

What had
happened? A hole
cut in the ice had bar
frozen over again, and then
the dog had fallen through.
Imagine looking the other way when
a thing like that happens (as people
sometimes do). Lying flat on my
stomach I groped through the hole
and finally got hold of a back leg

I dragged the dog out, rolled him in my coat, and ran home.

And then the Urban story:

because my wife and I had to go abroad, Amber and Urban had to stay in a kennel for three days. Arriving home we learned that Urban had gone — disappeared! I did everything that one could possibly think of, including consider the suggestion that we consult a clairvoyant.

This I did, at my wits'end. With some trepidation, I called a certain Mr. Tholen. He said, "I see the following landscape: a windmill without sails or something like that. With your back to the windmill there is a bridge over a canal on the left and just in front of you there is a field with sheaves of corn." There was more information about an unguarded crossroad, a small dike with little houses, and such. "There you will find your dog."

"And where would that be, Mr. Tholen?"

"About twenty miles northeast of your home." (I hadn't even told him where I was living!)

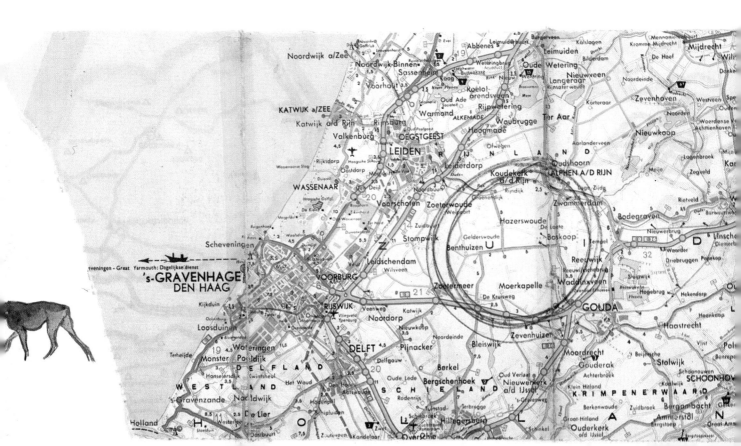

In all the nearby villages where I had advertised, I hung pamphlets everywhere, distributed them at schools,

bill from the local paper for the advertisement in the lost-and-found

stuck them on empty milk cans along the road, always keeping an eye open for windmills without sails (there are more of them than you'd guess).

Examining the horizon with binoculars I'd think, "Could that be Urban?" And going after it, I'd find nothing.

After five busy days of this, I came home to find a list of telephone numbers of people who had called.

"You have Urban at your house?"
"Absolutely," they'd say.
"A brindle male Boxer?"
"Absolutely."
And then there would be the disappointment I felt when I saw that it wasn't Urban at all, and didn't even look like him.

One short week after my telephone
call to Mr. Tholen: walking to the umpteenth windmill — without sails —
I feel to my surprise the strange sensation of blood rushing
to my head. For no particular reason I put the
pamphlet in the letterbox and I see that the
doorplate says: POORTVLIET

With a funny, whirly feeling, I turn quickly
and see Urban. I could only see
his head, the rest of him being under
a haystack, about 350 feet away.

A bit unstrung. I calmly approach him, softly calling his name.

But the dog flees, splashes into the canal, and I see the small dot disappearing on the horizon.

With nothing gained I return home and immediately telephone Mr. Tholen, who says, "A few miles farther on I see some sort of water tower, and next to it a barn where a motorbike is being repaired. You should go there!"
Confident of success, I went looking and found it!
The people there thought the story rather funny when I told them about Urban.
"No, we haven't seen anything."
But I wasn't home for a minute before the telephone rang: the mechanic said Urban had been caught!

Should anyone say he doesn't believe this story, I would fully understand. But, cross my heart, not one word of it has been made up. On the day that the landscape with the windmill was described to me Urban still had a long way to go before he got there.

In the vet's waiting room a nasty, globular little dog is yapping nonstop, teasing Urban. Sitting between my knees, Urban starts to growl. With the inside of my foot I let him know that he has to stop it. The owners had already been suspiciously eyeing Urban, who was in a sad state after his long adventure, and now the cup was overflowing:

"Sir, do you consider yourself an animal lover?"

The spoiled, stuffed animal was then pulled onto a lap and the three of them beamed forth strong distaste: "We have never kicked an animal!"

Well, I do consider myself an animal lover, but if a dog is willfully naughty it gets a backside kick (provided it has a firm bottom and of course only with the inside of your foot).

People sometimes have funny ideas about "animal love"; they think that excessive stuffing with cookies and such, or putting "nice things" around the cage has something to do with "animal love."

Well, they should know that a parakeet much prefers a fellow sufferer in its cage

and that, given the choice, this little terrier would rather be in a pigpen chasing rats than be perfumed and primped with curlers and brushes.

to a load of those stupid plastic playthings,

Once I saw someone in the waiting room who made the most of his "animal love."

He had devised a kind of upside-down saddle with carrying straps... that way the little animal would somehow have a much longer life.

I also saw → something like this somewhere

Somebody once brought me a duck that had swallowed a three-hooked grapple; you could even feel it! Because the poor animal was more dead than alive, I immediat... broke its neck.

And then that face people make: how could you do such a thing? Some people would rather see you fool around with an animal than put it out of i misery... a little artificial leg here, a plastic duc bill there, and if necessary, wheels attached to it — anything is better than dead.

"No, I couldn't do that!" Well, what good is tha to a cat in pain, run over by a car?

It is sometimes such an "animal lover with clean hands" who drives on.

I know those types who say, "How can you possibly shoot a roebuck But where does that fur coat, that snakeskin bag, come from? She doesn't care. You also mustn't bother her with stories of where veal cutlets and chicke breasts come from.

She has never struck one animal.

Just the same, what a thrilling question for a puppy: to whom will I be sold?
At Mr. L'Albee's (from whom we bought Manasse and who breeds longhaired, shorthaired, wirehaired, and and miniature Dachshunds) there was a lady who wanted a dog. "What kind of dog, madam?" Well, she thought she wanted one to match her coat. He sent her away without delay.

There is too much fooling around with dogs.

Because Hansje managed to pass his school tests, he was given a little dog, as promised. But after some time Hansje tires of taking care of the dog— besides, there is the new living room furniture — so Blackie goes to Uncle Wim's house.

But at his house when the baby starts crawling the dog is supposed to be "unhygienic" (after all, an animal so close!). Uncle Wim begins to regret the whole business.

But not to fear... Mr. de Jong is afraid of thieves and can use the dog!

And so on... because when de Jong closes his shop he no longer has need for a watchdog

Here are a few "unforeseen" circumstances:

the dog sheds,
it's small as a puppy but grows too big,
the dog had puppies,
the dog has a bad back,
you cannot breed it,
it constantly strays, etc.

Often they are the same "unforeseen" circumstances that cause people to take their dogs to the for an "injection." And as their summer vacation approaches they suddenly think th they cannot carry on with this dog anymore.

But then after vacation you might see them again, requesting worming preparations, only this time with a new puppy.

A puppy is so easily bought — for instance, to make a beautiful woman more beautiful, or to give a somewhat unspectacular person more stature.

(With a dog like this, sunglasses must be worn on the head.)

There are some men who are the underdog the whole day at work, with no say whatsoever:

not to the assistant supervisor,   not to the supervisor,   not to the president.

But then in the evening:

Tarzan here!!
Tarzan sit!!
Tarzan down!!

And then he secretly peeps over his paper to see if the dog stays down, lying like a block.

He also enjoys it very much when the dog frightens others: "for me he behaves like a lamb."

Many big dogs are purchased for this hobby. And don't forget another favorite pursuit: the possession of as many ribbons and trophies as possible.

No... hobbies enough!

They wouldn't want to miss their dog for all the world!

I am going to look for more models.

Here's a dog nobody
outside the Imperial
family of China was
allowed to possess,
the Pekingese.

This little animal with the flowing coat is the Maltese, an ancient miniature breed.

Pug

This flat little face
also comes from China.
It's said to have been
the favorite pet of Prince William
of Orange.

The
orded
ungarian
li

a little rascal out of Mexico.
weighing no more than 6 pounds,
the Chihuahua

A dog story Jan Hendriks once told me —
so I don't know for sure if it is true.

He is in a shop where his
fiancée is looking for a dress
or something. Getting bored, he
looks outside.

There he sees two women engaged
in a lively conversation. One has
a little dog on a leash. A
roadmaker working there
is getting pretty
annoyed by that
little dog, which is
yapping and teasing
him.

A few times already the
man has pushed the
thing out of the way

but it keeps on barking, incessan

The next swipe does not turn out well—it was not meant to be that hard—but the dog is <u>dead as a doornail</u>.

Without hesitation the man swiftly undoes the leash.

One quick grasp and that enormous hand puts the dog in the loose hand, tile on top:

tap — tap - tap.

A tip from a gamekeeper: if you lose your dog when taking it for a walk (really lost—no hammer work this time) then you should take off your socks or a sweater and put it where you lost him.

There is a good chance that you will find the dog waiting there the next morning.

the wolf gray
Keeshond
and the

Pomeranian

Cavalier
King Charles
Spaniels

A black Labrador
is really my idea
of a dog.

To continue in black:
from Flandres,
Belguim, comes the
Schipperke.

The Newfoundland is a
dog that adores the water—
in Newfoundland it helps
to pull the fishing nets
ashore.

the Chinese dog with the
blue tongue and masses
of hair, the Chow Chow

I like to watch people walk their dogs, because there are so many variations:

the jogger

the lounger

the romping boy

There are people who like to take a brisk walk...

and those who try to frighten the dog into relieving itself at the front door

.... people who let matters get out of hand by letting out a bitch in season.

This situation could likely become an "unforeseen" circumstance.

And during your walk with the dog you might "happen" to find yourself somewhere,

or you might casually see something →

or you might just bump into a friend ↓

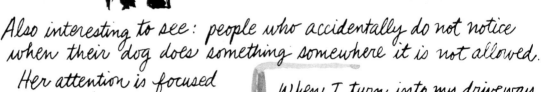

Also interesting to see: people who accidentally do not notice when their dog does something somewhere it is not allowed.

Her attention is focused on her handbag (but she knows perfectly well what her dog is doing on the pavement).

When I turn into my driveway, then there it is again, aiming at my ivy.
Its master stares fascinated by the clouds.

This is the dog's typical squat.

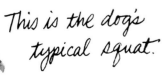

The Foxhound
often likes to chase
something else for
a change.

A keen and sharp little dog
that belongs to the boar hunt
is the German Hunt Terrier.

A still youthful Sep

How different can the march of events be from what is expected!
As we were trying to get used to the idea that sometime
we will have to say goodbye to old Sep, our dear
Max dies.

Just like that.... a heart attack;

for two days
he tried his best
and that was it.

No faithful
watchman
anymore in
the window,
no rap-knock-
knock anymore
with that tail.

It might be that the recently dug-up earth
is simply a comfortable place for Sep to
nestle, but the fact remains that he lies
there for long stretches,
and he never used to lie
there before.

You can see that Tim is not bothered ↗
by anything.

People who have never owned an animal find it hard to
understand a family's intense grief when their dog dies.
For such purposes I've already dug a few holes:

Urban lived only to six years old-
brain tumor;

Our first Sep didn't grow very old - three!
Weil's disease, in spite
of regular vaccination

Amber lived to be
pretty old - fourteen
But by then he w...
completely worn ou...
we had to
help hi...

The first dosage was accompanied by a biscuit,
which remained dangling out of the corner of his mouth.
I can still see the mischievous face of young Sep as he passed by
thinking, "Hey, a biscuit!"
Dumbfounded, we looked on as he snatched it away...
and happily trotted on.

It's a pity that a dog is with us for such a short time.

We drove to Luttelgeest, where the Kuiken family had a nest of German Wirehaired Pointers. We fell completely under their spell,

something you can do nothing about.

We chose this little fellow, and within two weeks he'll be old enough to come home with us. "Just choose a name that begins with an E."

The request took us by surprise. On the spur of the moment we couldn't think of anything else but Ezechiël, and in the car on the way home we thought it ...was not that bad.

EZECHIËL it shall be.

We await him, well equipped with the ever-present scraper and rolls of paper towels.

For use as a scraper I strongly recommend a fish slicer because it's so flexible — you just skim up the whole mess out of the carpet.

We always work in two shifts: I do the initial scraping, after which Mrs. Pootvliet comes with the detergent.

If the dog simply wets, it's much easier: thinly paper the area then rock heavily from heel to toe and back — that's all. _____

Actually the puppy could come home now — it's already eight weeks old — but first we're going to Ouddorp for two weeks. It's our vacation for pigeon and duck hunting.

I'm curious to see how he'll get along with old Sep!

And so our vacation is over and Sep has had, just as we did, a fine time.

Of course the most important news is that Ezechiël is here!

↙

We would liked to cuddle him right away, but it's better that the dogs are the first ones to get acquainted with him.

Old Sep has adjusted to him best so far. No problems.

Tim is fairly reasonable about it. But once in a while the young one pushes him too far—

Tim does _not_ like this kind of horseplay from behind.

↙

Manasse is acting silly— he is offended by
Ezechiël's presence,

and to show us how much he
suffers because of it he starts
to walk with an affectation.

Ezechiël has received little
affection from the two
Terriers.

At night when he is finally peacefully
asleep, twitching now and then with
growing pains,

I sit and look
at him with admiration.
How much this puppy has borne:
losing his mother, living in a
strange house where jealous little
dogs constantly growl at him,
and time after time that
rotten "NO!"

Pulling the cord of the vacuum cleaner: NO!

Blithely urinating indoors: NO!

Chewing the chair leg: NO!

Tearing up the newspaper: NO!

...ting the ...: NO!

Hiding fresh horse dung under the cushions: NO!

Teasing a brainless chicken: NO!

And after all that he still has not lost his spirit.

Right from the beginning it's been going very well.
He doesn't complain or whine; only when the alarm clock rings
in the morning does he get up. Then I have to arise at once
and lift him out of his
sleeping kennel. I
carry him downstairs,
through the garden
door, and after a
few steps outside
Ezechiël wets so
abundantly that it
becomes terribly
infectious!
The garden door can
be left open all day
so he can go in and
out himself, which
makes things a lot
easier than trying
to train a puppy
indoors in winter.

So that worked out beautifully. The only bothersome thing is that almost every morning I find a "protest puddle" from Manasse at the bottom of the stairs. Now how do I prevent that?

With a lively little jump-about like that in the house, you really have to watch what you're doing.

Then we have a snack, eating with our plates on our knees, we have to pray with our plates high in the air ("The lifting up of my hands in prayer," Psalm 141:2).

Together we are as happy as can be with the new member of our family!

Taking another good look at him, I think he could end up looking very much like Chris' dog

(next page).

German Wirehaired
Pointer
(bitch)

Our last hunting trip with Sep went better than expected. At first I just waited to see what would happen. However, I didn't even consider going for a bird that, when hit, might fall into a potato field or a field covered with heavy, tangled growth. That would have been too taxing for Sep.

After a rather long drought there was only 4 inches of water in the creek, but even that was rough on the old dog.

Since he hardly had the strength to wade through the mud, we left.

Jan's dog Cora had no difficulties with that — but then she's only eight years old.

This was an easier job for the old boy.

high reeds

dry drainage ditch

field of peas

cultivated land

ditch

If only I could let the pigeon pass overhead first, retrieval would be a cinch.

Actually, the dog should also hide in the ditch — the pigeons were able to spot him from a long way off... but Sep is old, and beyond the law. We'll leave it at that.

Although once again a wood pigeon would make a turn and fly off — he would sit there whining miserably when nothing happened.

When he finally did have to perform, the little drainage ditch gave him problems.

On the way down he was very cautious; his ascent was laborious—

but he made it nevertheless.

As he came closer I saw his old face beaming; he was proud as a peacock! After the bird had been handed over, he tried, while making a variety of faces, to get rid of the loose feathers. I helped him to do this with a splash of water from a bottle brought specially for this purpose.

So there he sits, pleased with himself, yet tired, while I occasionally shoo away pesty green flies.
(Sep has an old-dog bump on his head, and flies are attracted to it.
The other day I put bug repellent around it, which helped.)

Watching Sep retrieve a duck, I remembered something that happened this past spring: Sep comes innocently trudging out of the front yard without noticing a mother duck and her brood wandering in the area. Thinking that the dog has come too close she furiously jumps on his back,

which brings a loud howling from Sep, especially when the scruff of his neck was twisted.

Quite a surprise for an old gun dog.

Sep in his younger days

During our vacation the family Van der Veen came to visit us to show us their new young Labrador. It's always amusing to see how bewildered grown dogs act with such a tiny, outspoken pup around.

Sep, Tim and Manasse think this is very impudent →

Let's have a closer look at the little fellow.

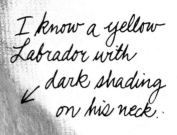

I know a yellow Labrador with dark shading on his neck.

When Amber, the young Lab,
arrived he immediately started
playing with the other pup,
turning over and over,

chasing each other without
watching where they
were going —

tumbling
into the reedy
growth of the
pond and coming
too close to the
ponies.

When they finally came in, we all of a sudden had five dogs in the house. Tim and Manasse weren't too happy about that.

Manasse would just love to be a puppy again.
If Sep has a bone, for example, Manasse will just "happen" to lie down right next to it; after a while he rolls over and then stealthily moves closer. And as soon as Sep looks away for a moment, the little one rolls over again — only this time on top of the morsel.

It's a typical trick that only a pup is allowed to get away with.

Since we've had Ezechiël, I haven't seen Manasse do this any more.

ook at the childishly protruding tongue!)

Not yet recovered from the Ezechiël mystery, Tim an
Manasse received another blow. My wife simply
could not do without a wirehaired Dachshund
after all:

GIDEON

Mrs. l'Albee brought
us the tiny
bundle last
Sunday

and our suspense ended when she placed
the small animal on the floor.

We watched Tim carefully
to see that he
behaved —

if not, there would have been the devil to pay.

ts fascinating to see the reactions to Gideon:

Manasse is sitting at a safe distance, muttering and cursing;

Sep is thinking that as long as he is left in peace, he won't object to anything.

n can barely ept the thing a dog. Perhaps doesn't want to, either.

chiël, still only three months old, thinks it is a toy cially for him.

When those two are romping together, you constantly hear Gideon's high-pitched yelps of fear. The jealous terriers cannot stand that; right away they stand over them in a threatening manner! We sure had to watch them all carefully those first few days!

You cannot blow a balloon up forever; one day it will burst!
You certainly do not have to be a dog psychologist to know that you have to be careful.

There is a danger of causing dogs to have a sour personality!

Gideon's lack of cleanliness makes for a rather unpleasant situation — yards and yards of paper towels are used, and when by chance he goes outside he doesn't even realize the excessive praise is meant for him.

Notice that Ezechiël's stance is flagrant,

but this requires a sharp eye (you can best spot it by the position of the tail

In the morning, just out of bed, when we walk into the shrubby front yard, I do not possess such a sharp eye and I therefore have to take care that I do not trip over the small creature.

Actually we are busy avoiding him all day, constantly watching where we s

People who cannot see their own feet have to stay away for a while.

It's a wonder that at this distance we're able to communicate with each other!

I held a yardstick next to him; the little guy is 5½ inches tall and I am 6'2½". So my height ÷ 5½" = 13 times bigger.

Imagine it the other way around —
6'2½" × 13 = 80'7".

It would take a lot of courage to stand there and wave to a creature about 80 feet tall.

He is so tiny that often you don't even see him — this morning I found him sleeping in between my sketches for the previous few pages of this book.

One thing for sure: this is going to be one who won't let the food be stolen from his plate!

Ezechiël is a good deal
bigger and heavier, but
Gideon doesn't give up easily.

that ferret
snout

A few times every day, however,
Ezechiël gallops straight into
him —

which is a bit
more than he
can withstan

The idea was that portraying different breeds would help with the choice of a new dog.

But because of the sudden death of dear Max, we didn't have a chance to think for long, and we ended up with a German Wirehaired Pointer and a wirehaired Dachshund again.

And, praise the Lord, that's how we all got together.

(braaf = good dog.)

We are very pleased with our new friends and have confidence
that in time everything will work out as it should...

not like this morning:
Gideon couldn't wait till we were
outside and began wetting as I
carried him downstairs;
my arm was
sopping!

When I came down later, washed and changed, to look
for my glasses, I found them under the table
with Ezechiël.

It wouldn't be difficult for someone who
hates dogs to make a convincing list
of minuses:

Gideon, using the
outside facilities for
a change, walks back
through his excrement and into the house;

Ezechiël affectionately licks my face, when just
a moment ago I saw him outside picking at a
half-decayed little bird;

and those terrible smells
that come out of the
dog basket
at night.

the pillow

the lawn

First in the pond,
← and then indoors
shaking out the water —
and drenching everything.

Something we were not aware of:
  after Ezechiël has had something to drink, about half a cup of
  liquid remains in his beard —
              ↙
                    that does not keep him from nestling comfortably
                                          down next to you
                                          on the couch.

It doesn't matter
much to us — we are
more or less dressed "adaptably," but we're fearful
      of what may happen to well-dressed visitors!

As a matter of fact, a few days ago we had visitors who had to wait quite a while until their dresses were finally clean and dry again — what a mess!

Truthfully, this is just a bad joke — these women never really paid us a visit. We did welcome this woman. She actually has nothing to do with a dog book except that when she was here she was sitting so beautifully with Tim on her lap.

We do have to get him out of the habit of jumping on people.

I met another breed again: the blue terrier from Ireland: the Kerry Blue.

Just a word of advice from our vet: beware of these narrow bones— more than once he's had to saw them off the lower jaw!

It's puzzling: one minute a dog is fast asleep in front of the stove, and the next he's happily running outside in the cold.

How can it be that he doesn't get sick?

His owner has to do all this before he's ready.

On this page I'm going to draw NIK.

In the first place I want to stay on good terms with Corry Kleyn; in the second place, to praise Amivedi,

the organization that found Nik (as they did so many other dogs) when he was lost,

and third, to show that a "mutt" in no way has to be less nice, sweet, intelligent, and whatever else you can think of than a purebred dog.

Some types of crossbreeding can
result in splendid dogs—
this beautiful dog is from a
German Shepherd and a Saint Bernard.

In order to draw the different breeds accurately,
I've been to many homes—a rather
interesting experience in itself.

I've entered houses in which I've almost
broken my neck stepping over
all the dogs...

and houses that have a doggy smell so thick
you could cut it with a   knife.

Upon ringing the doorbell you might be
confronted by something like this.
(Happily, there was thick glass
between us.)

There are big, small, friendly, and suspicious dogs,

dogs that reign supreme
in their homes;

dogs that greet you with
overflowing warmth,

and dogs that must have been afraid
that I would greet the owner too warmly.

Occasionally I would be advised not to move a muscle for a while...

it also happened once that I had to stand in the penalty-kick position for a long time.

Some dogs insist that they first get a couple of good, strong, jovial whacks on the back (at least that's what their owners maintain).

I am not so generous with those....

My little niece Renée, who is five years old, discovering the identification number tattooed in Gideon's ear, said, "Aunt Corrie, the price tag is still on!"

Another time I had to wait a good fifteen minutes before Poochie had conquered all fear sufficiently to come to the surface again...

And even though all this didn't help me in choosing the new members of the family, it furthered my general education nevertheless. I have become a little wiser again!

My heartfelt thanks to dogs and dog-loving people

THE LITTLE DOG

How grateful is my little dog
For small bones and some bread!
He wags his tail as round and round he walks,
And then he jumps upon my lap.

People give me meat and bread and wine,
And often a delicious sweet,
But if an animal can so grateful be,
What should people expect from me!

Hieronymus van Alphen

*(That shows you the kind of food
these good animals used to get i
those day*

Editor: Joan E. Fisher
Calligraphy: Diane Lynch

LIBRARY OF CONGRESS CATALOGING IN PUBLICATION DATA
Poortvliet, Rien.
  Dogs.
  Translation of: Braaf.
  Summary: Presents illustrations of many
varieties of dogs and includes information on
their history, physical characteristics, behavior, and uses.
  1. Dogs—Pictorial works. [1. Dogs] I. Title.
SF430.P7813 1983   636.7   83-7074
ISBN 0-8109-0809-3